WILD GOOSE PRINTS

no. 4

DEPICTIONS OF PEOPLE AND PLACES ON THE WAY TO THE CROSS

JOHN L. BELL & GRAHAM MAULE

These scripts are all intended for use in worship. All are firmly rooted in the Gospel narratives of Jesus' road to the cross.

First Published 1990

CONTENTS

The Wild Goose is a Celtic symbol of the Holy Spirit.
It serves as the logo of Iona Community Publications.

WILD GOOSE PUBLICATIONS
The Publishing Division of The Iona Community

Pearce Institute, 840 Govan Road, GLASGOW G51 3UT
Tel.(041) 445 4561 – Fax.(041) 445 4295

 ISBN 0 947988 35 1

INTRODUCTION

This book of scripts, unlike the previous three, has little recourse to humour. It concerns what are perhaps the most profoundly dramatic parts of the story of Jesus life – the events leading to the cross.

But, as with our other material, there is no requirement here for those who use the scripts to be well versed in religious drama – in some ways that can be a positive disadvantage. For here, the people portrayed are ordinary people, not actors, and the scripts allow them to tell their part of the story in direct and sometimes very simple language.

Most of these scripts were originally used in very conventional church buildings (fixed pews, elevated pulpit etc.) which had no previous history of 'dramatic' presentations. All we did, to enable the words to come alive, was to stop thinking in traditional church terms about how everything must happen at the front, and instead use the galleries, the side aisles, the walls and occasionally the pulpit to let events portrayed become an all round experience.

In so doing, as has been proven elsewhere, we discovered that the part of a church from which voices are best heard is not necessarily the pulpit, but sometimes under the gallery . . . the very place which presumption rather than evidence had made out to be the worst place from which to speak.

The scripts move from the declaration by Jesus that he is going to Jerusalem, to his sentencing by Pilate. Not everything involved in that period is covered, nor is there material on Jesus' resurrection appearances. We hope to include such material in future books.

For those interested in new songs for use during Lent and Easter, we suggest that items in the *Wild Goose Songs Vol.2* might be worth looking at, if hitherto they have been unknown to you.

We offer this book in the hope that those who use its material may be drawn close to Christ as they re-present his Passion.

John L. Bell
Graham Maule
February 1990.

HE WAS GOING ON A JOURNEY

This script is best suited to Passion Sunday.

It requires six readers, five of whom are placed around the circumference of the group or congregation. Only the person reading Jesus' part need be at the front or centre.

The script is in five sections, each of which has a similar shape. The four voices (A,B,C,D,) should follow each other in quick succession, the one beginning as the other says his or her last word. There should then be a short pause before the Narrator speaks, and Jesus' words should be direct and calm, in distinction to the frenzy of the first four voices.

There is a longer pause after each section. The effect might be heightened by having a drumbeat or a repeated note on a glockenspiel played at these points.

The value of the script is also improved if it is neither introduced nor commented on. It is enough to precede and follow it with an appropriate hymn, song or incidental music, e.g. it could be preceded by 'Oh where are you going?' *(*Wild Goose Songs Vol.1*) and followed by* 'Ride on, ride on the time is right' *(*Wild Goose Songs Vol.2*) or the more conventional* 'Ride on, ride on in majesty.*'*

Readers: VOICE A
VOICE B
VOICE C
VOICE D
NARRATOR
THE VOICE OF JESUS.

* * * * * * *

A : He was going on a journey . . .

B : He was going on a journey . . .

C : He was going on a journey . . .

D : He was going on a journey . . .

A : And Peter said,

B : And Thomas said,

C : And Andrew said,

D : And Judas said,

A : Where are you going?

B	:	Who is this man?
C	:	Which of us is greatest?
D	:	Lord, is it me?
NARRATOR	:	He was going on a journey, and Jesus said,
JESUS	:	Come with me.

(a pause)

A	:	He was going on a journey . . .
B	:	He was going on a journey . . .
C	:	He was going on a journey . . .
D	:	He was going on a journey . . .
A	:	And a young man said,
B	:	And a blind man said,
C	:	And a lunatic said,
D	:	And a leper said,
A	:	What must I do?
B	:	Take pity on me!
C	:	What do you want with us?
D	:	Lord, make me clean!
NARRATOR	:	He was going on a journey, and Jesus said,
JESUS	:	Do you want to get better?

(a pause)

A	:	He was going on a journey . . .
B	:	He was going on a journey . . .
C	:	He was going on a journey . . .
D	:	He was going on a journey . . .
A	:	And a woman in the crowd said,
B	:	And a woman at his side said,
C	:	And a woman at the well said,
D	:	And a woman on the road said,
A	:	Happy the womb that bore you!
B	:	Yes, it was me who touched you.
C	:	Can I have some of your water?
D	:	Lord, have mercy upon me.

NARRATOR	:	He was going on a journey, and Jesus said,
JESUS	:	I will be with you always.
		(a pause)
A	:	He was going on a journey . . .
B	:	He was going on a journey . . .
C	:	He was going on a journey . . .
D	:	He was going on a journey . . .
A	:	And John's disciples said,
B	:	And his home congregation said,
C	:	And the Pharisees said,
D	:	And the Chief Priests said,
A	:	Are you the one who is to come?
B	:	Could this be the carpenter's son?
C	:	Why does he eat with the outcasts?
D	:	From where do you get your authority?
NARRATOR	:	He was going on a journey, and Jesus said,
JESUS	:	I have come that you might have life.
		(a pause)
A	:	He was going on a journey . . .
B	:	He was going on a journey . . .
C	:	He was going on a journey . . .
D	:	He was going on a journey . . .
A	:	And the crowd were ready to say,
B	:	And the crowd were ready to cry,
C	:	And the crowd were ready to shout,
D	:	And the crowd were ready to scream,
A	:	Hosanna!
B	:	Blessings!
C	:	Barabbas!
D	:	Crucify him!
ABCD		*(shouted repeatedly and simultaneously and getting gradually louder)*
	:	HOSANNA! BLESSINGS! BARABBAS! CRUCIFY HIM!

NARRATOR : Jesus was ahead of his disciples
who were filled with alarm;
the people who followed behind were afraid.

So Jesus took the twelve aside and said to them:

JESUS : We are going up to Jerusalem
where the Son of man will be handed over to the chief priests and teachers of the Law.

They will condemn him to death
And then hand him over to the Gentiles
Who will mock him, spit on him and kill him;
But three days later, he will rise to life.

Come, let us go forward.

* * * * * * *

STAGES ON THE WAY TO THE CROSS

These stages represent different aspects of Jesus' journey towards the cross as seen by a variety of bystanders. The nature of the building in which the script is used will, to some extent, dictate the way in which the words can best be communicated. But here are two examples of how it has been employed:

1. In a large inner city parish, at morning worship, the seven readers were situated behind the congregation. This enabled those who were apprehensive about reading in public to lose some of their nerves. After each reader had finished, the organ played a solo line from one or other of the passion hymns, such as 'When I survey the wondrous cross.' *During the music the reader brought forward to the front of the congregation something which would be required for making a cross (nails, a hammer, a saw, rope, two large planks of wood etc.) and left it in a central location.*

2. At a large evening youth event in a contemporary church building, seven large posters were prepared which depicted the activities alluded to in the script. These were hung on the walls of the church, from the back, around one side towards the chancel where a wooden cross stood.

Each poster had a 'spotlight' (an anglepoise lamp) focussed on it. The chant 'Miserere Nobis' *(see* Goose Songs 3*) was sung as the sanctuary lights dimmed. Then, one by one, the spotlights lit up the posters while the readers said the appropriate words. After each reading, the light was extinguished and the chant sung once. At the end, all eyes had moved from the back of the church to the cross at which time prayers were said.*

It is important that, however the script is employed, the voices should sound natural. The range of characters represented allow for a good cross section of any congregation or group to be used.

Characters: FARMER
PHARISEE
TRADER
PRIEST
WORSHIPPER
JUDAS
LABOURER

* * * * * * *

FARMER : You have it coming to you.
You cannot traipse around the country
with a dozen vagrants,
some of whom can't speak properly,
and expect to be believed.

Your 'disciples' . . . if you can call them that . . . .
are common.
Your 'company' . . . which you choose to dine with . . . .
is common.
And you,
with your stories of lost coins and runaway children are
far from sophisticated.

People want a Messiah.
Not a former tradesman.
If you pretend to be the one,
but are the other,
you must take the consequences.

(a sung response, verse or music)

PHARISEE : You have it coming to you!
There is a time for playing the fool.
There is a time for poking fun
at what is serious in politics and religion.
But there is a border line between jesting
and indiscretion
which you obviously don't recognise.

Riding on a donkey,
with your starry eyed friends
throwing the shirts off their backs in front of you,
and doing this in 'royal style' . . .
that may be quite a laugh after dark,
when the streets are empty apart from drunk men.

But not,
not in the light of day
in the most sacred week of the year.

Those who do that
must be prepared for the consequences!

(a sung response, verse of music)

TRADER : You have it coming to you.
The police saw you,
the priests saw you,
the people saw you . . .
and though they cheered
don't be deluded.

'The Temple is the house of prayer' –
Who would disagree?
But if so, why scatter pigeons and pound coins
all over the place?

Of course, if it's sensationalism you're after
you are going the right way about it.
You might say the people
are more important than sparrows.
But send holy doves scurrying into the air,
and soon you'll discover what's really sacred.

(a sung response, verse or music)

PRIEST : You have it coming to you!
The place of worship is not a laboratory.
It is not for experiments.
It is not for seeing how far you can go
before someone shouts, 'No further!'

People sit still.
They listen to the Word.
They listen to the preaching.
They do not move
nor were they ever meant to.
And certainly, those who look worst
never seek the limelight.

But you . . .
You ask sick people to come forward.
And so they come,
with their withered arms and scabby faces,
lining up as if for a freak show at a circus.

Healing?
Oh there is a place for healing.
But not here!
Not here!

(a sung response, verse of music)

WORSHIPPER: You have it coming to you.
You are taking God into the market place
without permission.
You sit with the unemployed
and pretend that God is there.
You kneel down beside a whore
and pretend that God is there.
You smile at soldiers, heathen soldiers,
and pretend that God loves them.
You cannot do this to God.
You cannot take him where you want to go.
Worse still –
you cannot say that he is there already . . .
unless, of course,
you don't believe in the God we believe in –
in which case we have nothing to learn,
but plenty to teach you.

(a sung response, verse or music)

JUDAS : You have it coming to you.
And I am going to help it happen.
Three years I have watched you,
listened to you,
copied you
and have been let down.

For at the moment when you could have triumphed,
at the time when you had the crowds
eating out of your hand;
whenever people were ready for something big,
what do you do?

You chicken out;
away into the hills for a wander . . .
slink down a side street,
say 'Enough . . . enough . . . there will be another time!'

Well the time is coming.
I am your stage manager,
and I have negotiated my fee.

In a little while
the eyes of all will be on you.

Then you'll show them who you are
and what you can do.

And afterwards my thirty pieces of silver will buy a
good carry-out
for yourself and the boys.

(a sung response, verse or music)

LABOURER : You have it coming to you.

You don't know it
but this wood is for you.

Now being a carpenter
you could do lovely things with it . . .
turn it, dovetail it,
sand it down.

But we can't
for we're not carpenters.
We're not even joiners.
We're just labourers
earning a shilling on the side.

But we've been told
to keep quiet about our business.

So, without giving anything away,
but seeing as you might be who they say you are,
we'll let you know that
we're making something beautiful for God.

Ha, ha, ha, ha.

* * * * * * *

WOMEN ON THE WAY

Since at Easter we celebrate how women were the first witnesses of the resurrection, it is appropriate to remember them in our preparation for the festival.

This script retells the stories of four women who showed the kind of faith in Jesus which he did not always find in men.

Each biblical incident is followed by a reflection either by the women concerned or by another interested party.

It is recommended that this script be used either as the basis of discussion or meditation. To enable that, it is suggested that the script be read with people sitting, if possible, in the round. A table in the centre should have four small unlit candles at different corners. After the biblical narrative, a symbol, appropriate to the women depicted can be placed next to the candle. After the reflection, the candle is lit.

It is best that one person places the symbols on the table and that the other person, or the reader of Jesus' part, lights each candle.

A verse of a hymn or song or a chant such as Taizé's 'Ubi caritas et amor' *or the Iona Community's* 'Kindle a Flame' *might be sung as the candles are lit.*

One appropriate way of following the script is to move into a time of prayer where the leader simply asks people to pray for women, using the categories alluded to in the script.

Characters : NARRATOR
JESUS
MARTHA
WOMAN AT THE WELL (Noreen)
HAEMORRHAGING WOMAN (Cassie)
DISCIPLE
JUDAS

* * * * * * *

A. THE WOMAN IN THE KITCHEN

NARRATOR : Jesus and his disciples came to a village
where a woman named Martha welcomed him to her house.
She had a sister named Mary,
who sat down at the feet of the Lord
and listened to his teaching.

Martha was upset over all the work she had to do,
so she came to Jesus and said,

MARTHA : Lord, don't you care that my sister has left me
to do all the work by myself?
Tell her to come and help me!

NARRATOR : Jesus answered her,

JESUS : Martha, Martha,
you are worried and troubled over so many things,
but just one thing is needed.

Mary has chosen the right thing
and it will not be taken away from her.

(DUSTER placed centrally)

MARTHA : Well, that's my gas in a peep.
And for what?
For doing my best!

You know what it's like when somebody comes –
you hoover the carpet,
you brush the stairs,
you get out the wedding china . . .
    it's amazing the dust it collects
    even in the display cabinet –
you make sure there's a nice magazine at the fireside
. . . . the People's Friend or the Woman's Own
. . . . well you don't want them to know you read the
    Sun, do you?
And then there's baking to be done
and I never get pancakes to rise if I'm in a hurry.

And mother always told us when we were lassies
that when a visitor came,
to put on a clean peenie . . . apron, that is.

So I'm in the middle of all this
and I'm up to 99
and our Mary's sitting like a lodging house cat
and...

JESUS : Martha, did you hear what I said?
The dust and the pancakes and the scatter cushions
will come and go.
And there will be more housework and baking and
tidying up to take their place.

In the middle of your panic,
have you no time for something that will last?
Or is your whole life going to be devoted
to what frustrates you
rather than to what might transform you?

(CANDLE LIT)

B. THE WOMAN AT THE WELL

NARRATOR : Jesus came, by himself, to Jacob's Well in the town of Sychar. He was tired and sat down about noon.

A Samaritan woman came to draw some water
and Jesus said to her.

JESUS : Can I have a drink of water?

NARRATOR : The woman answered,

NOREEN : You are a Jew, I'm a Samaritan.
How can you ask me for a drink?

JESUS : If only you knew what God gives
and who was asking you for a drink,
you would ask him and he would give you life-giving water, and you would never be thirsty again.

NOREEN : Sir, can I have some of that water?

JESUS : Go and call your husband and come back.

NOREEN : I haven't got a husband.

JESUS : You're right.
You've had five,
and the man you have now isn't your husband.

NOREEN : I see that you're a prophet.
And I know that when the Messiah comes,
he'll tell us everything.

JESUS : I am he, I who am talking with you now.

(PITCHER placed centrally)

NOREEN : Well what could I say?
Harry's lying in his bed,
waiting for me to come back and make the dinner,

and I'm standing blethering to another man . . .
another man! . . . as if I'd not had enough trouble with men.

And he's a Jew.
And you know what Jews are like.
They'd rather eat a slice of streaky bacon
than talk to the likes of me.
To tell you the truth,
I've never spoken to one of them before.
Well, I mean, they're dirty.
They never do the dishes or wash their faces on a Saturday, and they think they're a cut above the rest.

But this Jew . . .
– I wonder what Harry would say if he heard I was talking to a Jew –
Anyway, this Jew . . .
I don't think I've ever talked to a man
who understood me.
I mean, men don't understand women,
but this man understood me.
It was as if everything I've never been able to tell Harry,
I could tell him . . .
even the things I don't like admitting to myself.
It was just like saying the best prayer of my life,
and having it answered there and then.

(CANDLE LIT)

C. THE WOMAN IN THE CROWD

NARRATOR : As Jesus was walking along,
people were crowding him on every side.
Among them was a woman who had suffered terribly
from severe bleeding for 12 years.
She had spent all her money on cures,
but instead of getting better, she got worse.
She heard about Jesus, so she tried to get near him,
saying to herself :

CASSIE : If I just touch his clothes, I'll get better.

NARRATOR : She touched his clothes and her bleeding stopped at once.
And she had the feeling, inside herself,
that she was healed of her trouble.
At once, Jesus knew that power had gone out of him,
so he turned round in the crowd and asked,

JESUS : Who touched my clothes?

NARRATOR : His disciples answered,

DISCIPLE : You see how many people are crowding you!
Why do you ask who touched you?

NARRATOR : But Jesus kept turning round to see who had done it.
The woman realised what had happened to her,
so she came, trembling with fear, knelt at his feet,
and told him the whole truth.
Jesus said to her,

JESUS : My daughter, your faith has made you well.
Go in peace, and be healed of your trouble.

(BANDAGE placed centrally)

CASSIE : You don't know what it's like.
You don't know what it feels like
and you don't know what it's been like.

Most women are bothered with bleeding once a month.
I bled every day,
every day for twelve years.

Some days I would just lie in my bed
and try not to stand up.
But it never worked.

Nor did the doctors.

I've been from doctor to specialist,
haematologist to gynaecologist;
and always the same questions:
How long have you been like this?
When did it start?
What brings it on?
Your family history? . . . Your diet?

I became a medical curio,
someone on whom the doctors tested their theories
and tried the latest drug.
And I realised that to them
my disease was more important than me.
But what cured me was finding the man
who believed that I was more important than the disease.
And all I did
Was reach out to touch him.

(CANDLE LIT)

D. THE WOMAN WITH THE GIFT

NARRATOR : Six days before the Passover,
Jesus went to Bethany, to the house of Lazarus.
They prepared a dinner for him which Martha helped to serve, and Lazarus sat close to Jesus at the table.

Then Mary took half a litre of very expensive perfume made of pure nard.
She poured it on Jesus feet and wiped them with her hair.
The sweet smell of the perfume filled the whole house.

At this, Judas said :

JUDAS : Why wasn't the perfume sold for 300 silver coins
and the money given to the poor?

NARRATOR : He said this, not because he cared for the poor,
but because he was a thief.
He carried the money bag and helped himself from it.
Jesus said to him

JESUS : Leave her alone!
Let her keep what she has for the day of my burial.
You will always have the poor with you
but you won't always have me.

(PERFUME placed centrally)

JUDAS : I don't care what he says,
I think it's a waste.

But, of course,
it's a habit of his.

Wherever there's something going for nothing,
he takes it.

I've seen us just walking into a town
and some heathen asks him
to come in to his house for a meal.

So in he goes and plunks himself down,
and then comes away with some rubbish about
how you have to receive what the poor have to offer.

This is a pretty good week for getting treated.

On Sunday he got a civic reception,
banners, big cheers, the works.
Yesterday the children sang for him
and he was as pleased as punch.
Tonight he's getting a four course meal
and perfume on his feet.
And I have got it on good authority
that somebody has laid on another banquet for Thursday.

But draw all this to his attention
and he'll excuse the extravagance without a thought . . .
'the gifts of the poor . . . the gifts of the poor'

It makes me sick.

If that stupid woman gave me her perfume,
I'd show her how it could stretch a lot further
than round his ankles and on to the carpet.

I could feed the poor

and buy her a bracelet with the money,
and she would have that long after he's dead.

(CANDLE LIT)

* * * * * * *

MAUNDY THURSDAY

As its title suggests, this script deals with the incidents leading up to the evening before the crucifixion. It is a review of some of the main events of Holy Week and is frequently used as a prelude to the sacrament of Holy Communion.

At its first performance, in the English Reformed Church in Amsterdam, the chancel area looked in disarray with upturned tables and chairs. It was from this location that the stall holder spoke and, at the end of the script, during a hymn, the characters rearranged the furniture and laid the tables, enabling the sacrament to flow from the action.

Not all the speaking, however, should be done from the front.

The Narrator and Jesus should be at the back of the congregation, Jesus being unseen until, at the end, he walks forward to wash Peter's feet.

The Cynic may speak from an upstairs gallery, a good place in which to be an onlooker, or from a side aisle. The Stallholder, if not speaking from a disordered chancel, may stand beside an unturned table in another side aisle or against a wall.

Towards the front left should be four chairs facing away from the congregation on which the Pharisees can sit throughout or during an interlude before their speaking part begins. Towards the front right should be another four chairs on which the four disciples can sit. Of these four, two may be Peter and Judas, and a third the disciple who begins the script. At the point at which it is alluded that the disciples went to the house of Simon the leper, the chairs should be turned inwards in order that Jesus may be seen to wash Peter's feet.

No particular dress is required for the script, though it is helpful to have the four Pharisees identified with each other either by similar costume or a common accoutrement . . . e.g. the same tie or scarf.

It is not advisable to try to do the script in 'period costume' as this inevitably makes it look like something which took over where the church nativity play left off. It also gives the impression that the events of Holy Week are for yesterday not today.

It is, however, advised that music be used to link the various scenes. It may be sufficient to have the Passion Chorale *(*O Sacred Head Sore Wounded*) played sensitively between each section. But that can only happen if the organist can play sensitively and the organ does not make heavy respitory sounds when not being played, which prevent the dialogue from being heard.*

An alternative might be to get someone to play that or another tune on the recorder. Or the choir (better still the congregation) might sing an appropriate chorus or chant between the scenes. Examples would be either the Russian Orthodox or a Taizé 'Kyrie Eleison'*, or* 'Wonder and Stare' *from* Wild Goose Songs Vol.2.

To use music in this way enables the script to become more of a shared experience than a spectacle, and to allow the congregation to be – in whatever small way – representative of the crowd which watched and followed Jesus in Jerusalem.

DISCIPLE : *(walking from back to front, as if in anguish)*

No, Jesus, No! *(wheels round to congregation*
and directs speech to Jesus at back)

Hardly three years . . . that's all we've known you,
long enough to want to keep you to ourselves,
long enough to know we share you,
but not to lose you.

No,
Not the miracles . . .
not the quietened storm,
not the fish that fed five thousand,
not the withered arms turning strong . . .
these – all right, they're important –
but they're not why we follow you.
It's YOU
YOU . . . that's why we're here.
That's why this unsophisticated crew
of half-baked fishermen and non-events
trail behind you.

You said 'Come.'
And not knowing where or why,
we followed;
And now,
just when everything begins to fall into place,
just when our eyes are beginning
to recognise who you are,
you want to end it all.

Do you want to die, Jesus?
Or is it heat?
Or has the pressure of the crowds
scared off your sanity?

Look,
forget the Passover.
There'll be other years,
and besides
we've all been there before.
What do you say?

(stands and stares at Jesus)

JESUS : We're going up to Jerusalem, and when we get there, I'll be handed over to the chief priests and scribes. They will sentence me to die, and hand me over to the Romans to be killed. They will mock me and spit on me and flog me with their whips and kill me:
but after three days I will come back to life again.

(MUSIC – during which disciple moves away.)

CYNIC : I cannot say I was very impressed, were you?
Or perhaps you didn't see it –
the royal procession, I mean.
We're used to processions in this city,
and demonstrations.
All it needs is some foreign princess
or secretary of state to come for afternoon tea,
and the crowds gather . . . .
lining the route, blocking the streets, waving madly,
and all desperate to get a wave back.

But this thing, this today,
was worse, much worse.
It was all rather disgusting and . . .
cheap? Yes . . . cheap!
Why the crowds went off their heads,
I don't quite understand
nor do I want to.

Oh yes, I caught a glimpse.
I do live above the main street after all . . .
I could hardly help hearing the racket.
I looked out . . . and there it . . . he . . . was.

A young man on a young horse on a hot day.

Poor fool.

I don't know who put him up to it,
but whoever was responsible
must have a very perverted sense of humour.

Our city has enough fools in it
without adding to their number
or giving them a king.
Everybody, of course, is talking about it . . .
the people here have such a taste for scandal.
I just hope that by now someone has rescued the poor
devil before he's put up to something more serious.

(MUSIC)

NARRATOR : Jesus went up to the temple and there he found the dealers in cattle, sheep and pigeons, and the money lenders at the tables. He made a whip of cords and drove them out of the temple, sheep, cattle and all. He upset the tables of the money changers, scattering their coins. Then he turned on the dealers in pigeons.

JESUS : Out! Take them out! You must not turn my Father's house into a market. It is to be a house of prayer for all nations. But you have made it a robber's cave!

STALL HOLDER : *(leaning on upturned table)*
Twenty years I've had a stall here
and my father worked in the temple before me.
We've had some weird types in our time
and we've had arguments . . . O yes, we've had
arguments. But never an outrage like we had today.

In comes this stranger with his friends and a whole crowd of children, and the next thing we know he's running about shouting and knocking everything everywhere. I mean, quite apart from anything else, someone could have got hurt . . . and what an example to show the children.

You see this table . . . it's my table. Half an hour ago it was covered with what I had to sell. Pigeons for . . . God I suppose . . . But I don't ask questions, I'm just here to make money.

The trouble with him of course, is that he doesn't respect tradition. That's it . . . he doesn't respect tradition. We have a way of working in this place. We've got a religion that's been going on for much longer than this building and it's what people like. It's what they're used to. You can't just burst into a church and tell them that they've got it all wrong.

I mean, religion is all about tradition, isn't it? Religion's not meant to change. People need something in their lives which is always there. That's why this building is here. That's why I'm here selling things to keep the people happy.

Why the police didn't come and arrest him, I'll never know. Some say they were afraid of public opinion, afraid there would be a riot. You see, he's well in with the crowd.

Now if he were a respectable, well educated man . . . I might have listened to him. But these upstarts from the working class with their funny accents. They don't know their place. Give them a bit of support and . . . .
and they think they're God.

(MUSIC during which Pharisees may move to their seats)

NARRATOR : Jesus left the temple and spent the night in Bethany. He returned to Jerusalem next morning and entered the temple. There the chief priests and elders of the nation came to him with questions. At the same time, Pharisees and lawyers devised a plan by which they intended to trap him with his own words, and they sent a delegation to join the questioning.

(The Pharisees stand up one by one as they speak directing their words to Jesus at the back of the building)

PHARISEE 1 : Jesus, by what authority are you acting the way you do? Who gave you that authority?

PHARISEE 2 : Jesus, haven't you said that we can't serve two masters? Then is it right to pay taxes to Caesar?

PHARISEE 3 : Jesus, isn't it true that you believe in the resurrection of the dead? Then can there be marriage in heaven?

PHARISEE 4 : Jesus, don't you claim to fulfil all the law? Then which is the greatest of the laws' commandments?

PHARISEE 1 : Jesus, who gave you authority?

PHARISEE 2 : Jesus, is it right to pay taxes?

PHARISEE 3 : Jesus. is there marriage in heaven?

PHARISEE 4 : Jesus, which law is the greatest?

PHARISEE 1 : Who gave you authority?

PHARISEE 2 : Is it right to pay taxes?

PHARISEE 3 : Is there marriage in heaven?

PHARISEE 4 : Which law is the greatest?

JESUS : *(shouting)*

ALAS ! !
Alas for you, lawyers and pharisees . . . . hypocrites !
You shut the doors of the kingdom of heaven in people's faces. You do not enter yourselves, and when others are entering you stop them.

Alas, alas for you, lawyers and pharisees.
You travel over land and sea to make one convert,
and when you have won him, you make him twice as fit for hell as you are yourselves.

Alas, alas for you.
You are like tombs covered with whitewash.
They look well from the outside, but inside they are covered with dead men's bones.

O Jerusalem, Jerusalem . . .
The city that murders the prophets and stones the messengers sent to her! How often I would have gathered your children as a hen gathers her chickens under her wings . . . . but you would not let me.

(MUSIC during which Pharisees resume their seats)

NARRATOR : Jesus told them a story . . . .

When the Son of Man comes in all his glory and all the angels with him, he shall separate the people of the nations into two groups, as a shepherd separates the sheep from the goats, and he will place the sheep on his right hand and the goats on his left. Then the king will say to those on his right hand :

JESUS : You have my Father's blessing; come, enter and possess the kingdom that has been ready for you since the world was made.

For when I was hungry, you gave me food; when thirsty, you gave me drink; when I was a stranger you took me into your home; when naked, you clothed me; when I was ill you came to my help, when in prison you visited me.

NARRATOR : Then the righteous will reply . . .

(standing and turning as they speak)

DISCIPLE 1 : Lord, when was it we saw you hungry and fed you?

DISCIPLE 2 : Lord, when was it we saw you thirsty and gave you a drink?

DISCIPLE 3 : Lord, when was it we saw you a stranger and took you in?

DISCIPLE 4 : Lord, when was it that we saw you naked and clothed you?

DISCIPLES : *(Together)* LORD, WHEN DID WE SEE YOU ILL OR IN PRISON AND CAME TO VISIT YOU?

NARRATOR : And the king will reply . . .

JESUS : I tell you this; anything you did for one of my brothers here, however humble, you did for me.

NARRATOR : Then he will say to those on his left hand . . .

JESUS : The curse is upon you; go from my sight to the eternal fire that is ready for the devil and his angels. For when I was hungry you gave me nothing to eat; when thirsty nothing to drink; when I was a stranger you gave me no home; when naked you did not clothe me; when I was ill or in prison you did not come to my help.

NARRATOR : And they too will reply . . . .

(standing and turning as they speak)

PHARISEE 1 : Lord, when was it that we saw you hungry?

PHARISEE 2 : Lord, when was it that we saw you thirsty?

PHARISEE 3 : Lord, when was it we saw you a stranger?

PHARISEE 4 : Lord, when was it we saw you naked?

PHARISEES : *(Together)* AND WHEN DID WE SEE YOU ILL OR IN PRISON?

JESUS : I tell you this: *(here they turn their backs)* anything you did not do for one of these, however humble, you did not do for me.

NARRATOR : And they will go away to eternal punishment, and the righteous will enter eternal life.

(MUSIC during which the Pharisees confer together in a corner and the disciples rearrange chairs to face inwards)

Then the chief priests and the elders of the nation met in the place of the high priests, and there they conferred together on a scheme to have Jesus arrested by some trick and put to death.

(Pharisees mumble to each other before speaking aloud)

PHARISEE 1 : It must not be during the festival.

PHARISEES 2, 3 & 4 : Why not?

PHARISEE 1 : There may be rioting among the people.

(they remain standing in a huddle)

NARRATOR : Jesus was at Bethany in the house of Simon the leper, when a woman came to him with a small bottle of fragrant oil which was very costly; and as he sat at table she began to pour it over his head. The disciples – or at least one of them – objected . . . .

(Judas withdraws from disciples and stands aside, moving eventually towards the Pharisees)

Then Judas Iscariot, one of the twelve, went to the chief priests to betray Jesus. When they heard what he had come for, they were greatly pleased.

JUDAS : How much will you give me to betray him?

(The Pharisees turn towards Judas and one of them clinks thirty pieces of silver into a purse during Judas's speech. All the officials look dour, directing their gaze at him. Judas speaks to the congregation, to himself, or to the Pharisees as the words suggest.)

There . . .
I've said it, I've said it,
I've said it.
And now . . . I feel much better.
It's a weight off my shoulders,
it's a burden off my mind,
it's a great relief . . . *(pause)* . . . Is it Hell!
It is Hell . . . and it's still Hell . . . and . . .

Well,
Somebody had to do it.

Somebody had to handle the dirty goods.
He has to die – he said it himself,
I'm only helping him on his way . . . on to a cross.

But who knows,
maybe he needs this.
Maybe this will rouse him to display
all the power he's supposed to have.

Maybe I'm doing him a good turn.
Maybe he'll even say 'Thank you Judas.'

Oh Judas! *(pause)*

Well they know I'm a thief anyway.
They know my reputation and so does he.
I may as well live up to my name.
After all, I don't claim to be the 'saviour of the world',
I just claim to be myself.
Anyone in my situation would do exactly the same thing .
. . . Wouldn't you?
. . . if the money was good enough?
. . . if you couldn't live with your jealousy?
. . . if you didn't know whether you were loved?

(to officials)

How much did you say?

(snatches money and looks at it)

Is that all?
Is that all he's worth?
Is that all the hell in my head is worth?
Thirty pieces of silver . . .

Just about enough to buy a piece of rope to hang myself
and a burial plot for my body.

I'm only joking of course. *(re piece of rope)*
Of course I'm only joking. *(re betrayal, offering money back)*
Of course I'm only joking. *(beseeching to give back, but officials point to the door)*

Of course . . . . *(hesitates, stumbles, runs out)*

NARRATOR : On the first day of unleavened bread, when the Passover lambs were being slaughtered, his disciples said to him

DISCIPLE 2 : *(standing and speaking)* Where would you like us to go and prepare for the Passover supper?

NARRATOR : So he sent two of his disciples with these instructions:

JESUS : Go into the city and tell a certain man "The Master says 'My appointed time is near; I am to keep the Passover with my disciples at your house'"

NARRATOR : The disciples did as Jesus directed. They prepared for the Passover and in the evening he came to the house with the twelve.

(Music during which Disciple 1 and 2 go outside. They may return with bread and wine if appropriate.)

NARRATOR : Jesus knew that his hour had come that he must leave the world and go to the Father. He had always loved his own who were in the world, and now he was to show the full extent of his love. During supper, Jesus, well aware that the Father had entrusted everything to him, and that he had come from God and was going back to God, rose from the table, laid aside his garments, and taking a towel, tied it round him. Then he poured water into a basin and began to wash the disciples feet and to wipe them with the towel.

(During the last sentences Jesus walks from the back with a towel and a basin and as he nears the front, Peter rises, Jesus stands motionless while Peter speaks and during part of the Narrator's speech)

PETER : You're not going to wash my feet.
You're not going to wash my feet!
I mean it, and I won't let you.
It's not your job, such dirty work.
It's not your place to be seen doing
what masters love and servants loath.
And I – we – have come to call you master;
and you – YOU – want to be our servant!
Oh how humiliating!

You are the one we call our Lord.
You are the one on whose own word
all our words hang.

You are the one we'll always follow,
the one we'll never reject,
never betray, never deny.

Oh why empty yourself of dignity
to go down on the ground like a slave?
If you're down on your knees
Won't the world walk on by,
thinking you feeble and weak?
Why not rule from the sky
stretch your arms round the world
not my ankles?

You're not going to wash my feet!
You're not going to wash my . . . .

NARRATOR : *(interrupting)*

Peter,
This is what he must do.
And this is what you must let him do.
To prevent it . . . is to pretend to be perfect,
and you are in as much need of washing as us all.

(Pause while Jesus approaches and Peter sits. The following words are said as water can be heard washing Peter's feet)

This, whom you call 'servant', is your Lord.
To be the Lord means to be the servant;
to do the dirty work, and to do it in love.

And that is very costly, although you count it stupid.

For a good world, a man may lay down his life with pride;
but for a bad world
and for people who reject, betray, deny,
it is much harder.

His power is in his weakness.
And you may not know that today,
and you will not think it tomorrow
when from a cross, against the sky,
he hangs helpless.

But this is the way the world is transformed . . . .
  by loving the unlovely,
  by dying for the lifeless,
  by forgiving those, like you,
  whose hearts are too stubborn to see
  what they are or know who he is.

Be still, and let your feet be washed
    and let your mouth be closed.

Think not always to act,
always to speak.
But first let your Lord do for you
what you must do for each other.

(Music, possibly a hymn during which the chancel is prepared for the celebration of Holy Communion.)

* * * * * * *

THE TRIALS

Jesus was not merely tried before Pilate, the political authority. He was first tried before the Sanhedrin, the Jewish religious court.

This script allows both trials to be represented. It is not literal nor does it exhaust the possibilities of dramatising the courtroom scenes, but it attempts to make clear a) that Jesus was sent to his death by religious people, b) that false accusations were framed against him, c) that in fulfilment of prophecy, he had committed no sin nor did he defend himself with anything other than the eloquence of silence.

A traditional reformed church building with a high pulpit and a reading desk or lectern is ideally suited for the script.

Pilate should be out of sight either in a side balcony or in the pulpit. Caiaphas needs to occupy a slightly less elevated central position . . . the pulpit or a raised dais on which an imposing chair may be positioned.

The witnesses can read from a lectern, angled so that their voices are projected to the congregation. Alternatively, they might be placed sitting among the congregation.

The Narrator reads from the back and Jesus, who only has one line, can either stand at the back or stand in the middle of the centre aisle.

Caiaphas and Pilate can be dressed in some kind of religious or civic garb and Jesus, dressed ordinarily, may have his hands tied behind his back.

The introductory passage to be read by the worship leader may be omitted or amended as desired.

CHARACTERS: NARRATOR
JESUS
CAIAPHAS, HIGH PRIEST
SHABBETH, AN INFORMER
JOLBAD, AN INFORMER
ANNAS, FATHER IN LAW OF CAIAPHAS
PILATE, THE ROMAN GOVERNOR

* * * * * * *

LEADER : We have come on this night/day to remember –
to remember how the King of Heaven
was, on earth,
betrayed, rejected and sent to his death
by religious people who thought they were doing the right thing.

We have come knowing that we ourselves would have done the same.

But we believe,
and in the life of Christ we see,
that the love of God
is greater than the sin of the world.

That is the hope
which takes us through
the suffering and death of our Lord
to the joy of his resurrection.

NARRATOR : He grew up before the Lord like a young plant
whose roots are in dry ground:
he had no beauty, no majesty to draw our eyes
no grace to make us delight in him;
his form, disfigured, lost all the likeness of a man,
his beauty changed beyond all recognition.

He was despised, he shrank from the sight of people,
tormented and humbled by suffering.
We despised him, we held him of no account,
a thing from which people turn away their eyes.

Yet he himself bore our sufferings;
our torments he endured
while we thought he was punished by God,
struck down by disease and misery.

We had all strayed like sheep:
each of us had gone our own way.
But the Lord laid upon him the guilt of us all.

CAIAPHAS : *(stands)*
As High Priest,
I am the official guardian
of our traditional and orthodox religion.

It is my duty to investigate heresies,
and to discipline heretics
and any other who would pervert our faith.

I have been summoned this night
to investigate complaints against one,
Jesus, from the town of Nazareth, in Galilee.
So, let me hear the accusations.
Who are the witnesses for the prosecution?

(Shabeth goes to the lectern)

SHABETH : I am one, sir.

CAIAPHAS : Who are you?

SHABETH : My name is Shabeth.
I am a friend of Annas, your father-in-law.
I change foreign currency for visitors to our city.

CAIAPHAS : And what have you to say?

SHABETH : I have it here; *(brings out a paper)*
I wrote it down.

CAIAPHAS : Why?

SHABETH : In case I forgot it.
I want to get it right.
He . . . that man *(points)* . . . Jesus . . .
he said he would destroy the temple.

CAIAPHAS : What?

SHABETH : He said he would pull down the temple . . . destroy it.

CAIAPHAS : Did you hear him say that?

SHABETH : Eh . . . no . . . that is . . . not personally.
But I know someone who did,
and they told me, and I told Annas,
and that's why I'm here.

CAIAPHAS : And how exactly was he going to destroy the temple?

SHABETH : I don't know . . . but I've a good idea.
A lot of people know him;
a lot of people listen to him;
a lot of people follow him.
If they get hysterical . . . they'll do anything.

CAIAPHAS : Who are these people?

SHABETH : The lower classes, sir . . .
the crowds . . . the rabble.

CAIAPHAS : Anything else?

SHABETH : Well . . .
There was a rumour about him and a
servant woman from Bethany.
I'm not one for gossip
but I wouldn't be surprised if it were true.

CAIAPHAS : *(looks at Shabeth and nods, waves him down)*
Be seated.
Now who else?
Who else has information?

(Jolbad goes to the lectern)

JOLBAD : Me, sir.
I have information.

CAIAPHAS : Who are you?

JOLBAD : My name is Jolbad.
I am a friend of Annas, your father-in-law,
and I'm a cleaner in the temple.

CAIAPHAS : And what have you to say?

JOLBAD : Here it is.
I have it here. *(brings it out)*
I also wrote it down.
I did not want to forget.

Yes, *(looks over it)*
it says . . . .

That man . . . eh . . . Jesus.
he said he would build another temple.

CAIAPHAS : Build another temple?

JOLBAD : Yes . . .
in three days.

CAIAPHAS : Do you expect me to believe that?

JOLBAD : It's true, sir.
That's what he said.

CAIAPHAS : Did you hear him say it?

JOLBAD : Well yes . . . and no . . .
You see, I was standing on the edge of the crowd.
I could not hear everything.
I could only make out some words now and then.
So I asked a man who was standing closer
and that's what he told me.

CAIAPHAS : And you believed that man?

JOLBAD : Yes, of course.
He . . . Jesus that is . . .
he does tricks.
He does magic tricks;
he does tricks with fish and bread;
he does tricks with trees;
he threatens to move mountains and ruin our landscape.

Personally, I think he works for the devil.

He will build another temple in three days if he wants to.
But it will be the temple of Satan.

CAIAPHAS : Did he say that?

JOLBAD : Does he have to?
Isn't it obvious, sir?

CAIAPHAS : Anything else?

JOLBAD : Yes
I don't know if I should say this in such a place, but . . . .
he talks to prostitutes.
Oh yes, I know it for a fact.
I've seen the company he keeps.

CAIAPHAS : *(waves him down)*
Take your seat.
Who else?

ANNAS : There's me.
(Annas goes to the lectern)

CAIAPHAS : Your name please.

ANNAS : I am Annas.
I am your father-in-law.
I have much to do with our religion, like you,
and I have much to say about this man. *(opens his script)*
Firstly,
You have heard what he said about the temple.
I admit, the information is not clear.
But it is enough surely to convince you
that he is a threat to the life of our beloved institution.
Secondly.
He is a threat . . . to our national security.
We live at peace under the Roman government.
We pay our taxes, we behave responsibly;
we gain the benefits of Roman civilisation.
We respect Pilate, our Governor;
we respect Caesar, our Emperor,
although we don't worship him as others do.
We value the peace and the progress
we have in our country.
And then along comes this man
questioning Caesar's authority,
saying to the people:
'Give to Caesar what belongs to him'
. . . these, more or less, are his words.
Now, what have you that belongs to Caesar,
and what have I?

Do we have Caesar's furniture? Caesar's palaces?
Caesar's slaves, Caesar's books?

Of course not.

The conclusion, as I understand it,
is that because we have nothing belonging to Caesar.
We should forget about him.

But let us forget Caesar for one minute
and he will not forget us.

No . . . we will suffer for our lack of memory.

This man is a nationalist of the worst variety,
for he is a threat to our nation's peace.

And thirdly . . .
he is a threat to our religion
for he claims to be the Messiah.

This . . . this tradesman *(pointing)*
has been tricking the faithful of our religion,
turning their minds away from the true worship,
encouraging them to believe that
he and his philosophies were sent from God.

This . . . . this tradesman
and his twelve ignorant companions
have been encouraging immoral practices,
breaking the law of the Sabbath,
questioning the authority of the Priests,
preaching heresy . . . .

CAIAPHAS : *(Suddenly interrupting)*

Stop . . . Stop . . . *(he rises and moves angrily to the front)*

Is this true?
Is this all true?

Are you the Messiah?

(silence)

Speak, man ! ! !

JESUS : These are your words.

CAIAPHAS : These are my words?
These are your words ! ! !
These words are blasphemy.

Pilate! *(Yelled out. Caiaphas now goes to the lectern)*

PILATE : *(naively)*
Yes, Caiaphas?

CAIAPHAS : Your excellency,
This is the day before our Holy celebrations,
our Passover.

On this day our nation rids itself
of anything which is unclean or foul.

So on this day, I bring to you this foul man. *(points)*

I have no authority
to proscribe that punishment which is most fitting.
But in your hands there lies
the power to deal with him as he deserves.

PILATE : Why, what has he done?

CAIAPHAS : Three things . . .
He is a threat to our nation and our religion
for he questions and breaks our rules of faith.

He has opposed the payment of taxes to Caesar
and set himself up as a rival power.

He claims to be a King.
He says that he is our Messiah.
As High priest,
I know he is not.

But I fear the wickedness which may follow
if this man is left at liberty.

PILATE : Is that him? *(pointing)*

CAIAPHAS : That is him.
His name is Jesus.

PILATE : Your name is Jesus
and you've heard what has been said against you,
so what do you say in your defence?

(silence)

I repeat, you've heard what has been said against you.
Now what do you say in your defence?

(silence)

Look here, man . . . your life is at risk.
Are you not going to defend yourself?

(silence)

PILATE : *(exasperated)*
You have been brought to me on three charges.
These charges, these accusations
are made by your church.
Now, I'm not a Jew; I don't worship your God;
religious matters don't even interest me.

But because the Jews have no lawcourts of their own
I have to administer justice for them.

If it were an ordinary trial . . . .
if you had stolen some sheep or killed a man,
I would know what to do.

But religious heretics and Jewish Messiahs
only confuse me.

I have no complaints about you from the police or the army, only from your religious leaders.
In their eyes, not in mine, you are guilty.
If you can convince me otherwise . . . .
I am prepared to let you go.

Now what have you to say?

(silence)

What have you to say, man?

(silence)

(Pilate turns to Jews)

PILATE : Under Roman law, I cannot find this man guilty.
But if he has caused trouble to you and to your establishment,
I am prepared to have him flogged and set free.

JEWS : No ! ! !

PILATE : But what am I to do with him?

JEWS : Crucify him ! ! !

PILATE : Crucify your . . . King?

JEWS : *(all speaking at one time)*
He is not our King !
Who says he's our King?
Rubbish, lies, lies !

CAIAPHAS : He is not our King !
Caesar is.
And you . . . are Caesar's delegate.

PILATE : Then,
if he must be crucified,
he must be crucified.

In my hands lies the authority for his death
but in your hands,
I leave the responsibility.

(Pilate and Caiaphas remain motionless and look at congregation)

NARRATOR : He was afflicted;
he submitted to being struck down
and did not open his mouth.
He was led like a sheep to the slaughter,
like a ewe that is dumb before the shearers.

Without protection, without justice, he was taken away
and who gave a thought to his fate?
He was cut off from the world of the living,
put to death for the people's sin.
He was given a grave with the wicked,
a burial place among the rubbish of humanity,
though he had done nothing wrong
and said nothing which was untrue.

(characters leave in silence)

* * * * * * *

CURRENT PUBLICATIONS OF THE IONA COMMUNITY

THE WHOLE EARTH SHALL CRY GLORY		Paperback ISBN 0 947988 00 9
THE WHOLE EARTH SHALL CRY GLORY	Iona prayers by Rev. George F. MacLeod	Hardback ISBN 0 947988 04 1
THE IONA COMMUNITY WORSHIP BOOK	Iona Community	ISBN 0 947988 28 9
THE CORACLE = REBUILDING THE COMMON LIFE	Jubilee reprint of Foundation Documents of the Iona Community	ISBN 0 947988 25 4
PEACE AND ADVENTURE	Ellen Murray	ISBN 0 9501351 6 X
90 RECIPES FROM THE IONA COMMUNITY	Sue Pattison	ISBN 0 947988 17 3
RE-INVENTING THEOLOGY	Ian M. Fraser	ISBN 0 947988 29 7
MEANING THE LORD'S PRAYER	George T. H. Reid	ISBN 0 947988 30 0
PARABLES AND PATTER	Erik Cramb	ISBN 0 947988 33 5
HEAVEN SHALL NOT WAIT (Wild Goose Songs Volume 1)	John Bell & Graham Maule	ISBN 0 947988 23 8
WILD GOOSE SONGS = VOLUME 2	John Bell & Graham Maule	ISBN 0 947988 27 0
LOVE FROM BELOW (Wild Goose Songs Volume 3)	John Bell & Graham Maule	ISBN 0 947988 34 3
A TOUCHING PLACE	Wild Goose Worship Group	Cassette No.IC/WGP/004
CLOTH FOR THE CRADLE	Wild Goose Worship Group	Cassette No.IC/WGP/007
LOVE FROM BELOW	Wild Goose Worship Group	Cassette No.IC/WGP/008
FOLLY AND LOVE	Iona Abbey	Cassette No.IC/WGP/005
FREEDOM IS COMING		Cassette No.IC/WGP/006
FREEDOM IS COMING	Utryck	ISBN 91 86788 15 7
THROUGH WOOD AND NAILS	Iona Abbey	Record No.146/REC/S
WILD GOOSE PRINTS No.1	John Bell & Graham Maule	ISBN 0 947988 06 8
WILD GOOSE PRINTS No.2	John Bell & Graham Maule	ISBN 0 947988 10 6
WILD GOOSE PRINTS No.3	John Bell & Graham Maule	ISBN 0 947988 24 6
WILD GOOSE PRINTS No.4	John Bell & Graham Maule	ISBN 0 947988 35 1
EH . . . JESUS . . . YES, PETER . . . ? Book 1	John Bell & Graham Maule	ISBN 0 947988 20 3
EH . . . JESUS . . . YES, PETER . . .? Book 2	John Bell & Graham Maule	ISBN 0 947988 31 9
WHAT IS THE IONA COMMUNITY?	Iona Community	ISBN 0 947988 07 6
CO-OPERATION VERSUS EXPLOITATION	Walter Fyfe	ISBN 0 947988 22 X
COLUMBA	Mitchell Bunting	ISBN 0 947988 11 4
FEEL IT = Detached Youth Work In Action	Cilla McKenna	ISBN 0 947988 32 7
PRAISING A MYSTERY	Brian Wren	Hope Ref. 749
BRING MANY NAMES	Brian Wren	Hope Ref. 747